WOMEN
IN THE
MARINES

The Boot Camp Challenge

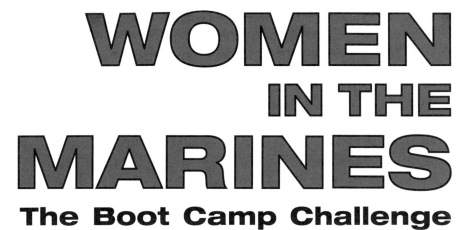

WOMEN IN THE MARINES
The Boot Camp Challenge

Written and photographed
by N. R. Rowan

 Lerner Publications Company ▪ Minneapolis

The material in this book was obtained by the author from his observations and interviews with recruits, instructors, and officers during four visits to Parris Island, South Carolina, from 1990 through 1992. Information was also obtained from conversations and documents provided by the Public Affairs Office, Marine Headquarters, Washington, D.C.

The author would like to thank Major Robert McClean, Major Scott Campbell, and Staff Sergeant Angela McDaniel of the Parris Island Public Affairs Office for their assistance with the manuscript, interviews, and photography. The author gives special thanks to Captain Todd Yeatts for reviewing the manuscript and offering invaluable comments and suggestions.

Library of Congress Cataloging-in-Publication Data

Rowan, N. R.
  Women in the Marines : the boot camp challenge / written and photographed by N. R. Rowan.
    p. cm.
  Includes index.
  Summary: Describes the experiences of female recruits at the Parris Island Marine Corps Recruit Depot and discusses the role of and opportunities for women in the Marines.
  ISBN 0-8225-1430-3
  1. United States. Marine Corps—Women—Juvenile literature.
[1. United States. Marine Corps—Women.] I. Title.
VE23.R69 1994
359.9'6'082—dc20   93-9706
                                                                     CIP
                                                                     AC

Manufactured in the United States of America

1 2 3 4 5 6 – P/JR – 99 98 97 96 95 94

CONTENTS

This book is dedicated to my parents, Grace DeLacey Kinsley and Roy W. Kinsley, for their understanding and support over the years.

This book is also dedicated to the 14 courageous women who lost their lives during the Persian Gulf War in 1991:

U.S. Army

Cindy Beaudoin, 19, Plainfield, CT, Medical Specialist
Cindy Bridges, 20, Trinity, AL, Motor Transport
Tracey Brogdon, 27, Bartow, FL, Florida National Guard
Beverly Clark, 23, Armagh, PA, Water Treatment Specialist
Tatiana Dees, 34, Congers, NY, Military Police
Dorothy Fails, 25, Taylor, AZ, Motor Transport
Pamela Gay, 19, Surrey, VA, Personnel Administration
Lorraine Lawton, 28, Lafayette, LA, Adjutant General
Christine Mayes, 22, Rochester Mills, PA, Food Service
Adrienne Mitchell, 20, Moreno Valley, CA, Equipment Specialist
Cheryl O'Brien, 24, Long Beach, CA, Avionics Mechanic
Marie Rossi, 32, Oradell, NJ, Helicopter Pilot
Kathleen Sherry, 23, Tonawanda, NY, Communications

U.S. Navy

Shirley Cross, 36, Fountain, FL, Aeriographer's Mate

Introduction

The Marine Corps is the United States military branch that specializes in amphibious (sea to land) assaults. Once an all-male fighting force, the Marine Corps is now open to both male and female recruits. Women make up approximately five percent of the 180,000-member Marine Corps.

To earn the right to be called a Marine, female recruits must make it through basic training, or boot camp, at the Parris Island Recruit Depot in South Carolina. Of the four military services—the United States Army, Air Force, Navy, and Marine Corps—Marine basic training is the longest and toughest, both mentally and physically, with the greatest emphasis on physical fitness and conditioning.

The drill instructors (DIs) at Parris Island are trained to be demanding. They constantly challenge recruits and push them to new levels. From day one, excuses are not tolerated here. In return for a sincere commitment to listen, learn, and train hard—the Marine way—recruits earn many personal rewards, including self-confidence, self-discipline, and self-reliance. The Marine Corps is not for everyone. But the personal rewards of being a Marine are substantial for those with the strength and motivation to reach the Emblem Ceremony at the end of boot camp.

This book will examine the boot camp experience, as well as the military careers that follow. Let's meet some brave young women of the Fourth Recruit-Training Battalion. They have sought a challenging and unconventional "rite of passage," with a significant level of difficulty and risk. For this alone they deserve our respect and admiration.

"Drill instructor shock." Night One—Recruit Monica Franklin meets her first drill instructor.

8

1
Welcome to Parris Island

"The males come here to Parris Island expecting the worst experience of their lives. The females come here expecting the most exciting challenge of their lives."
—Captain Todd M. Yeatts

It's about 3:30 A.M. on a cool Friday morning in November. A bus full of female recruits has just departed Charleston, South Carolina, for the Marine Corps Recruit Depot at Parris Island. The sleepy young women, ages 18 to 24, are about to experience what many will later say was the most exciting challenge of their lives.

At the Parris Island guard house, the bus is cleared for entrance. It logs in at 4:10 A.M.—make that 0410, military time. Most of the recruits are napping and will miss this transition from 4:10 A.M. to 0410. But the transition from civilian to military life—and the next 13 weeks of boot camp—will change the recruits' lives in ways they may not fully understand for years.

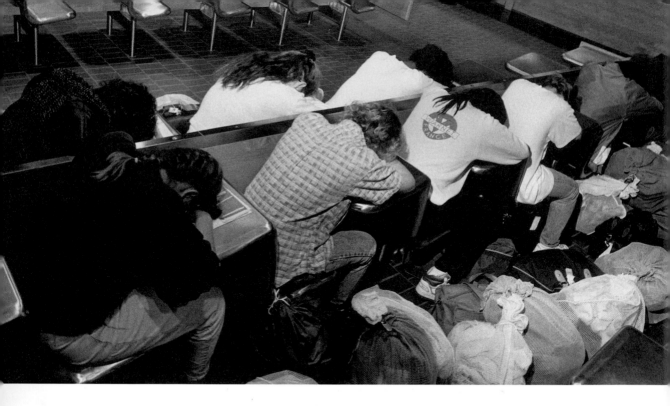

Top: Recruits wait
with their heads
down while their
forms are being
processed. Right:
Recruit Becky
Robison unpacks
personal items
she's brought to
boot camp. Most of
these items are
against regulations.
She will have to
mail them home.

As the bus comes to a halt, an impeccably dressed sergeant with a clipboard is waiting. She climbs on the bus and says, "Welcome to Parris Island." Recruits begin to stir and rub the sleep from their eyes.

Then all hell breaks loose! A volley of "You will"s comes right at the recruits like a series of 100-mile-an-hour hardball pitches. The young women face their first military weapon—a weapon of control—the power and sting of the Marine drill instructor's voice. The pace of the recruits' lives is about to be squared.

"You will, upon my order, disembark my bus!" the DI shouts. "You will have one minute to gather your belongings and line up on my yellow footprints! You will not talk! You will stand at attention, eyes straight ahead! You will disembark my bus now! Move!"

Wide-eyed and in shock, the recruits scurry off the bus in record time. Sure enough, painted on the ground outside the bus are rows of large, yellow footprints. The recruits quickly realize that the vacation they used to call their lives is now over.

The recruits are led from the yellow footprints into the receiving building, where they will fill out forms. There, in the processing area, a recruit asks for a pencil in the usual, civilian manner.

A sergeant immediately responds: "You will speak only when spoken to! There are no private 'I's! You don't say, 'I don't have a pencil'! You say, 'This recruit doesn't have a pencil, Ma'am or Sir'! You will place your head down on the desk when you finish your forms!"

Groups of female and male recruits, arriving on separate buses throughout the night, are led to the receiving building. For women, the processing procedure is somewhat shorter and less stressful than it is for the men. Women don't get the shaved-head haircut as men do, nor must they spend the first 48 hours at boot camp without sleep. Women will be led to their temporary quarters about four or five hours after arrival and will be allowed to sleep that night.

Why do the female recruits escape some of the harsher treatment that their male counterparts are subjected to on the first day at Parris Island? Many drill instructors say the women are better-motivated recruits and need less discipline than the men.

"I've been in the Marines for 14 years," says Sergeant Wayne Moore. "And I can tell you, the females listen up! They make better recruits overall than the males. They are better motivated, adapt better, take instruction better, and seem to retain what they learn better. I've never had a female recruit refuse to jump off the 45-foot rappelling tower. So far three males have refused to jump."

The first five days at Parris Island are spent in processing, receiving, and orientation. Recruits complete paperwork, receive uniforms and supplies, learn how to march correctly, how to store their equipment, and how to talk and ask questions like a Marine. For most, the adjustment to a military routine is very stressful.

"The first five days are the most difficult," recalls First Lieutenant A. J. Kozlowski. "You feel acutely disoriented, homesick, and alone. They move you in during the middle of the night, hustle you through processing and forming, and separate you from the people you came in with. The identity you came in with is quickly stripped away. You feel as if you are in nowhere land—no longer a part of anything."

Drill Instructor Sergeant Vanessa Bitterman makes sure that everyone learns the rules of conduct at Parris Island.

"This recruit woke up the first day here, and there were DIs swarming all around me, yelling," adds Cynthia Copeland, 20, of Keystone Heights, Florida. "It was very unpleasant. We were rushed out of our bunks, rushed to fix our hair, brush our teeth, use the head [bathroom], and get in line at attention in front of our bunks. All this in four to five minutes was a bit of a shock."

13

"We definitely stress them out to get their attention," explains Sergeant Vanessa Bitterman. "The DI's role is not one of a friend to the recruit.

"We have two basic tools to control and motivate. The first is the voice. We use it as a weapon of control. No one wants to be singled out in front of the group for criticism. Secondly, we use IPT: incentive physical training. Essentially this is disciplinary exercise like push-ups, sit-ups, and jumping jacks."

Recruits live in temporary quarters until "pickup," the Monday following their arrival. On pickup day, recruits move to the main barracks at the Fourth Battalion, where they meet their permanent drill instructor team—the three or four DIs who will guide the group through basic training.

"There is a point during the first week when you are assigned to a drill instructor and a unit for the duration of your stay," Lieutenant Kozlowski explains. "They call it pickup. You now become a part of something again. This is your new family—your new identity."

This new group of 40 to 45 recruits, called a platoon, will live and train together for the next 13 weeks. Reveille, the bugle call that wakes recruits in the morning, comes at 5:00 A.M. Lights-out occurs at 9:00 P.M. In between, recruits receive 14 hours of training with about 20 minutes allowed for each meal.

Drill instructors foster a healthy competition among platoons for the three major symbols of prestige at Parris Island: trophies for military knowledge, drilling, and physical fitness training. Recruits want to excel not only for themselves and their platoon, but also for their drill

14

instructors. They quickly learn to respect the DIs' ability and knowledge.

The DIs and the legendary sand fleas of Parris Island often team up to teach recruits self-discipline. During outdoor inspections, recruits must stand with their hands clasped behind them for long periods. They must not talk or move. The sand fleas, of course, take this opportunity to feast on any part of a recruit's skin that isn't covered with gear or a uniform. Should a recruit swat a flea or move a millimeter, a team of DIs will swoop down on her immediately. One recruit had 16 sand fleas on her hands, with 8 or 10 more on her neck and ears. She never flinched.

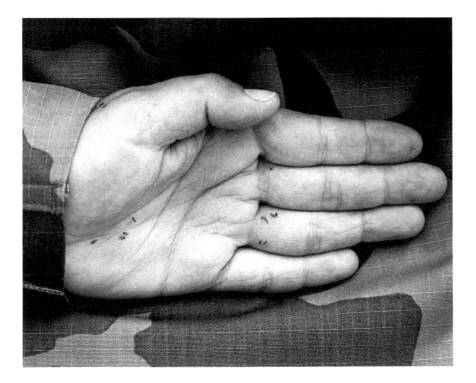

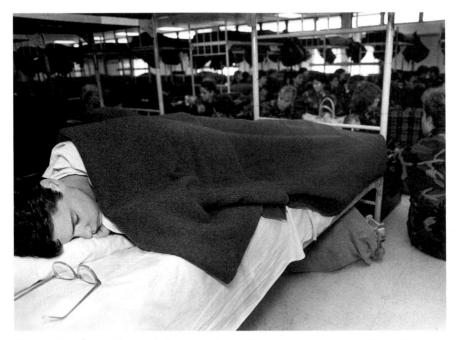

A recruit who collapsed during physical training recovers from heat sickness and dehydration.

On average, about 2,000 female recruits come to Parris Island each year. Not everyone will graduate, however. About 20 to 25 percent of the recruits will drop out before boot camp is over. Most (about two-thirds) of these leave for medical reasons, such as injuries. The others drop out for FTA: "failure to adjust" to military life.

Boot camp is a "survival of the fittest" situation. Those recruits who do survive will struggle, sweat, and work like they have never worked before. They will be pushed to the edge and past their old breaking points. One of the rewards of survival here is the development of positive self-esteem and self-confidence.

"Many of these young kids come here fresh out of high school," says Drill Instructor Sergeant Sandra Nails. "They've had it pretty easy up to now. We push them here like they've never been pushed before. We build confidence where there was none before. You can see the look of pride on their faces that says 'I did it! I did it!'"

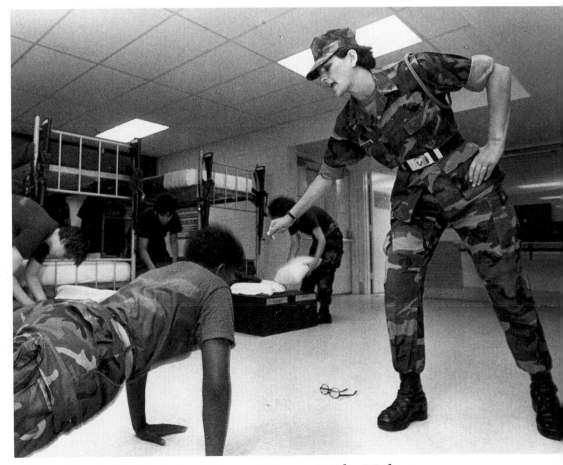

Incentive physical training: "Give me 20, recruit," the DI shouts.

2
The Boot Camp Experience

Basic training is divided into three phases—I: orientation, military drills, and PT (physical training); II: instruction with various weapons on the rifle range; and III: Basic Warrior (combat) Training.

During Phase I, which lasts for four weeks, recruits run, swim, do calisthenics, complete a five-event obstacle course, and take hikes with 5- to 25-pound packs for up to 10 miles. They also attend daily lectures on subjects ranging from first aid and sexual harassment prevention to military tactics, history, and customs. Recruits even learn the correct military application of cosmetics. Let's take a look inside a squad bay (barracks) during Phase I training.

Bunk Basics: "No Lumps, No Bumps!"

The pace this morning is frenetic. Recruits are learning to make a bunk bed the Marine way. "You see it once—you better get it right!" the DI yells.

The DI maneuvers around a demonstration bed pulling the sheets over the mattress and carefully folding the top sheet over a blanket. With a ruler, she measures six inches from the head of the mattress to the start of the fold. It all happens in a flash.

"You've got five minutes. No lumps, no bumps," she shouts.

There's a Marine Corps way to do everything—even make a bed.

"Move!" The recruits scramble for the pile of sheets and blankets on the floor. Working in teams of two, they tackle the top of the bed first and secure the sheets and blanket. Then they lie on the floor under the bed and tuck the blanket neatly all around. With 10 seconds left, the DI starts the countdown to what some of the slower recruits fear will lead to IPT.

Near Bunk 3, a recruit is down on the floor cranking out IPT push-ups. A DI hovers over her.

"That's an attitude, recruit," the DI yells. "You better get rid of it now, recruit! Now give me more sit-ups. . . . Now give me jumping jacks. . . . Now give me push-ups."

The recruit slows from fatigue, and she takes a breather in between orders. The DI, hands on hips, leans into the recruit's face and shouts: "Are you refusing to train, recruit?"

"No Ma'am," the recruit responds, hitting the deck again and pumping out more push-ups. Her violation? Wandering eyes during instruction.

Separating the Women from the Girls

The Confidence Course includes seven events. Two of the more difficult events are the Slide for Life, in which recruits shinny down a long rope angled high over a small, murky pond, and the Confidence Climb—up, over, and down a 39-foot log ladder.

It becomes very clear one morning how the Confidence Course got its name. Two DIs are running to assist a recruit on the Confidence Climb. She is one rung from the top of the giant log ladder but has become frozen with fear after turning to look down.

Many recruits say the Confidence Climb is one of the most challenging training events at Parris Island.

While the two DIs on the ground shout words of encouragement, two more DIs climb up the ladder to help the recruit. They do not bring her down, however. They coach her to complete the course herself. The recruit climbs over the top rung and down the ladder. Her platoon cheers as she reaches the ground.

Then the recruit asks permission to climb the ladder again! She reaches the top and goes over and down by herself. A glowing smile and new look of pride emerge on her face.

The emphasis during all the training events at Parris Island is on building confidence and self-discipline. Drill instructors will push a recruit relentlessly—until she overcomes any self-defeating excuses that are keeping her from completing a challenge.

Even if a recruit doesn't complete an assigned task, the DIs will push her to exhaustion—or until they are satisfied that she has done her best. The two worst offenses a recruit can commit at Parris Island are making excuses and giving up on a task before putting forth her very best effort.

23

Battle Sight Zero

In Phase II, recruits move to the Weapons Battalion barracks, where they receive two weeks of training with weapons, including the M16A2 rifle. To pass basic training, each recruit must score a minimum of 190 out of 250 points on a shooting test. Currently, a woman holds the Parris Island rifle-range record with a test score of 248 points.

Recruits first receive classroom instruction, then they practice firing weapons on the rifle range. They learn to adjust the rear sight of their rifle until the weapon is accurate at a distance of 300 yards. Rifle-range instructors call this setting "Battle Sight Zero."

Eighty percent of the women will pass the shooting test—with a score of 190 points or more—on their first try. If a recruit doesn't pass her first test, though, she will receive another chance later in the day—as well as the following week. One-on-one help is also available each day for recruits who need it. Instructors use a special electronic rifle

A rifle-range instructor helps a recruit hold her head at the correct angle during weapons training. Opposite: Recruits team up to operate the M60 SAW (Squad Automatic Weapon).

connected to a laser-aiming machine and a computer. The computer screen display shows a recruit how problems with her aim can be corrected.

Many rifle-range instructors think women are easier to train than men. They note that women learn faster during the classroom portion of rifle training. "The females listen better," one instructor says. "They seem to have a more intense attention span."

Even so, the average female recruit's rifle test score is 200 compared with the average male recruit's score of 212. What causes the difference? Sergeant James Berry, a statistician with the Weapons Training Battalion, has a theory:

"We find that the females score the same as the males during the first three parts of the test," he says, "but don't do as well in the latter two, where the prone [lying down] position is emphasized.

"This may be because the average female is shorter than the male, and they therefore have a shorter arm length on average, and it is more difficult for them to reach the trigger during the latter two prone shooting positions of the test. If you factor out the prone position shooting scores, the females shoot on average equally with the males.

"Last year, out of 1,231 females, only 11 were dropped from the Marine Corps for failing to qualify with the rifle. . . . That means that 99.1 percent of these females qualified."

Between Phases II and III, recruits receive a one-week break from training. They return to their original barracks and spend a week doing "mess and maintenance"— everything from sweeping floors, mowing grass, and shining brass to working in the mess (dining) hall and repainting training equipment.

On the "Slide for Life," recruits shinny down a rope angled over a muddy pond. About halfway through the course, they receive the order to flip over. They complete the course upside down.

28

Basic Warrior Training

During Phase III, recruits move into the field and live in Southeast Asia huts (SEA huts)—simple wood-framed shelters with large, screened windows. For the next 15 days, recruits receive Basic Warrior Training, combat training with grenades, gas masks, mines, booby traps, and various weapons. They also learn about biological and chemical warfare, defensive maneuvers, and squad tactics—how to work together as a team.

Morning classroom instruction covers subjects like day movement, camouflage, and concealment. Each afternoon recruits move into the field and apply what they have learned in the classroom. They learn how to work as a team and how to correctly carry the M16A2 rifle under all combat conditions. They practice moving forward in a coordinated effort called rushing. They also learn to scale a wall while under fire and how to crawl under barbed wire on their backs.

An infiltration course simulates combat. Loudspeakers blare out the sounds of battle, while recruits cross water-filled gullies on narrow logs, belly-crawl across smoke-filled fields, and maneuver under razor-sharp barbed wire. Every few minutes, sticks of dynamite explode in sandbag-lined pits to simulate incoming mortar, grenade, and artillery rounds.

On the grenade range, two platoons have just completed grenade instruction, including five practice throws with dummy grenades. Above, in a control tower, an officer issues instructions over a loudspeaker. All along the outside of the tower are deep gouges in the concrete from shrapnel—the sharp metal fragments released during a grenade explosion.

A recruit now stands with an instructor in a cement-block pit built into the edge of a high dirt wall. The instructor hands the recruit a real M67 fragmentation grenade. The grenade is "live"—it will explode seconds after it is thrown.

The recruit holds the grenade close to her body with the "death grip"—a firm, two-handed grip she has already practiced. She pulls the safety pin, cocks her throwing arm, and takes aim at a group of "enemy" dummies in the field beyond. Her goal is an accurate toss of at least 50 feet.

The recruit wings the grenade. Both she and the instructor crouch down behind the dirt wall. Seconds later there is an ear-shattering explosion. Shrapnel flies in all directions.

Recruit Shannon Barrett hurls a live grenade. Opposite: Shannon and the instructor take cover as the grenade explodes.

Pamela Jones of Charlotte, North Carolina, was beaming when she exited the grenade range. "The tower loudspeaker said 'good throw!'" she remarked. "I did it right and it was acknowledged. That's very satisfying to this recruit, Sir."

Were the recruits nervous when holding a live grenade? "No Sir," a recruit replies. "Everything we do here builds confidence."

Building Marine Character

Without question, some of the most difficult and scary—but exciting—training events are the rappelling and "helo-jump" exercises off a 45-foot tower. During these events,

31

most recruits face some personal fears and physical weaknesses. They also find and reinforce their physical and emotional strengths.

Imagine you are a young woman with no mountain-climbing experience. Like most people, you have some fear of heights. You are taken one morning to the base of a rappelling tower. (Rappelling is a mountain-climbing technique used to descend cliffs.) You receive about an hour of instruction on the ground, learning how to prepare your rope and harness.

You watch an instructor rappel down the steel-framed tower. Then you climb steps to the top of the tower, stand backward at the edge, secure your rope to your harness, and jump off, releasing only a few feet of rope. When your feet make contact with the vertical face of the wall, you bend your knees and spring away, releasing more rope as you go, to control the rate of your descent. You repeat the procedure again and again until you reach the ground.

Then you climb up again. This time you do the helo-jump—as if you were jumping out of a helicopter. You jump straight off the tower into thin air, give the Marine Corps yell—"Go Marine Corps"—and glide down on a rope in a semi–free fall.

The House of Pain

Phase III also includes a gas chamber exercise, which helps prepare recruits for a chemical attack. Many recruits say the gas chamber is the most difficult part of their physical training. Recruits privately call it the "House of Pain." Staff Sergeant Michael Ozimok explains:

A DI demonstrates the helo-jump technique.

"All the recruits learn to respect the gas chamber. First recruits 'don and clear' [put on and prepare] their gas masks inside the chamber while CS [Chemical Smoke—a type of tear gas] is being pumped in. If they follow their training with the mask and get it on and cleared correctly, they will be fine while the gas builds up. If not, they are in trouble, because their eyes are going to sting, and they will start to breathe in gas, and it's somewhat painful.

"Then, a few minutes later, the recruits are required to remove the mask, and for about ten seconds they must breathe the CS gas with the mask off. When we open the doors to the chamber, the recruits pour out one on top of the other, and it usually isn't a pretty sight. They're coughing, spewing mucus from their noses and throats, and feeling nauseous."

"Everything is stinging and burning when you lift your mask and break the seal," a recruit recalls. "It's pandemonium in there, with some recruits screaming and slapping the walls. It sounds like they are dying."

"The worst part is not knowing where you are because you can't see," another recruit remembers. "The back of my neck felt like a blowtorch was aimed at it. Your sinuses burn right away, and your eyes slam shut. It's even worse when they let you outside after the mask is removed, because your nose is running all over you, and you feel like you need to vomit."

One recruit couldn't get a tight seal with her mask in the chamber. The young woman was swallowing gas and in distress. A fellow recruit came to her assistance, and then her DI came over and started yelling at her. Did the yelling help or just make the situation worse?

34

Recruits exit the "House of Pain."

"Yes, it helped me because it woke me up," the recruit explained later. "I was panicked, and it got me back on track. We are a team, and I was thinking about myself at the time. I learned a valuable lesson, and I'm a better recruit because of this experience."

The House of Pain seems like a horrible experience, yet the recruits smile with enthusiasm as they describe it. "This recruit would like to say that everything here builds your self-confidence and your ability," one woman says. Five other recruits concur with smiles, nods, and "Aye Sir."

35

In the field, recruits break for lunch. Food comes from packs called MREs (meals ready-to-eat).

While the recruits lunch on rations, their DI summarizes the group's performance in the gas chamber. Her overall tone is supportive, with criticisms that are very helpful. She mentions the recruit who had difficulty in the chamber but does not single her out by name.

When the DI finishes her analysis, a recruit raises her hand and tells the platoon that she was the one who panicked. "This recruit would like to thank Recruit Smith," she says, "who helped her in the chamber. This recruit froze for a moment and was breathing CS. Recruit Smith helped me to get back on track."

Other recruits raise their hands and join in the discussion. Some women offer comments on ways to improve the exercise. The DI listens and thanks the recruits for their input.

"What you did here today is a test of your confidence in yourself and your equipment," she says. "You've got to learn to trust yourself and your equipment and your training with it."

"It is a lesson well learned," Sergeant Ozimok adds. "When you are in a biological-chemical warfare situation, don't panic, trust your equipment and your training, secure your position, and you will survive."

Line Training

Phase III also includes Line (linear infighting neural override) Training. Line Training teaches recruits basic self-defense techniques for combat situations and for rape prevention. "We have statistics that every three minutes a woman is raped," an instructor says. "One out of every four females has experienced a form of rape, most often date rape."

Line Training techniques include kicks, punches, stomps, and ways to use a knife against an attacker if necessary. At Line Training class one afternoon, two platoons of women are sitting on the grass in straight rows. All eyes are on male and female instructors who are demonstrating how to defend yourself against someone who has just grabbed you around the neck in a front choke hold.

The instructors break the defensive maneuver into steps. The recruits observe each step and repeat each command after the instructor: "Grip . . . twist . . . pull . . . grab . . . sweep . . . stomp."

"Good to go?" the male instructor says, making sure the recruits understand each portion of the technique before he continues. The recruits respond in unison with "Aye Sir!"

The recruits then pair off, face each other, and practice

the techniques they have just seen. One recruit lunges at the other. She yells "Kill!" as she grabs her victim around the neck in a front choke hold.

The defender twists the attacker's wrist into the "inverted L" position. She then executes a simulated forearm smash designed to break the attacker's arm at the elbow. Next, there is a simulated grab for the groin area. A sweep with the leg and foot knocks the attacker off her feet and slams her to the ground.

Each recruit on the ground is advised to cover her head with her arm before the defending recruit follows up with a simulated stomp to the head. The defender slams her heel into the sand, just inches from the other woman's head. Sand sprays into the attacker's face.

The instructor gives the "recover" command, and the defending recruit helps the attacker back on her feet. They switch positions and repeat the exercise.

Line Training for self-defense. An instructor (left) helps a recruit execute a kick. Opposite: a recruit applies the wristlock to her attacker.

Preparing for Graduation

During the last two weeks of Phase III, recruits return to their barracks to prepare for graduation. They take their last PT test and a drill evaluation. Their uniforms are tailored for a perfect fit (most recruits have lost weight during training). They undergo three inspections on three different days. The battalion commander's inspection is the final and most important inspection.

At the Fourth Battalion this afternoon, tension fills the air. Recruits are dressed in their formal uniforms. They stand in front of their bunks, facing each other in two columns, waiting nervously for the inspection team.

Sergeant Major John Mersino arrives with the Fourth Battalion commander. They will inspect each recruit on her hygiene, rifle maintenance, and military knowledge. They will check her uniform for loose ends, hanging threads, length, and fit. Each recruit's hair must be neat and must be pinned or braided above the bottom edge of her collar.

Sergeant Major Mersino is assisted this day by the platoon's DI, Sergeant Rachael Capeheart. Sergeant Capeheart has a clipboard resting on her hip. As Sergeant Major Mersino moves down the line, the DI will record his evaluations and his comments about her recruits.

Sergeant Major Mersino makes a right face (right turn) directly in front of a young woman, notes her name, and asks what she feels was the most difficult part of her training. "This recruit found Phase I to be the most difficult, Sir," the recruit answers.

While the recruit speaks, the sergeant major looks carefully at her posture and uniform. He checks the length of her skirt and hair.

The final inspection: Thirteen weeks of training come down to this moment.

Then Sergeant Major Mersino orders the recruit to "present arms." With a lightninglike swipe and a loud slapping sound, he pulls the recruit's rifle from her grip. He cartwheels the weapon clockwise to inspect the condition of the butt plate area.

But Sergeant Major Mersino's eyes see more than just the weapon. He is also carefully observing the recruit's military attitude and her demeanor under stress.

41

While he runs his finger inside the chamber of the recruit's weapon, he asks her the significance of the emblem she is wearing. Less than a second passes between her answer and the next question: "What is the fifth General Order? . . . Who assigns a sentry to a post?"

The sergeant major pauses for a moment and holds up a blackened fingertip. "What is this?" he asks.

The recruit hesitates. "Dirt, Sir."

The questions and responses continue: "What are the three types of court-martial? . . . Which is the most severe?" The sergeant major adjusts the recruit's collar and the angle of her cover (hat) while she responds to the questions.

Finally, the sergeant major turns to Sergeant Capeheart with his report: "Hygiene, above average; rifle, average; uniform, excellent; knowledge, excellent." As he moves to the next inspection, there is a quiet but noticeable look of relief on the first recruit's face and also in Sergeant Capeheart's eyes. This final inspection is also a reflection of her ability as a DI.

From Recruit to Marine

After 13 weeks of training, recruits have finally made it to the coveted Emblem Ceremony at the end of boot camp. They are in the best physical condition of their lives. They stand tall and proud in their dress uniforms and polished shoes. The Emblem Ceremony is a deeply rewarding experience for the recruits and their families.

When the ceremony starts, the Fourth Battalion commander introduces her staff and the graduating platoons to the audience of parents and friends. Recruits march to

military music onto the parade grounds and line up in two long, parallel rows. The commander acknowledges those recruits who have received special honors, awards, or promotions during basic training.

Then two senior officers move down each row, one recruit at a time. There are quiet words of congratulations while the officers pin the Marine emblem on each recruit's cover. After 13 tough weeks, the recruit has earned the right to be called a Marine for the first time.

3
Is the Marine Corps for You?

The requirements for acceptance into the Marine Corps are basically the same for women and men. Normally, a recruit must be a United States citizen. Under special conditions, registered aliens may be accepted.

Recruits must be between the ages of 17 and 28. They must hold a high school diploma or the equivalent. Female recruits must be no shorter than 4 feet, 10 inches and no taller than 6 feet, 6 inches—with weight proportional to height. They must be in excellent physical health and have no record of drug abuse or arrest for a serious crime. Recruits under 18 need the consent of both parents or a legal guardian before joining.

Enlistments are available in the Marine Corps for three, four, five, and six years. The minimum enlistment for non-technical jobs, such as Military Police, public affairs, or administration, is four years. Highly technical jobs, such as those in aviation and electronics, require longer training periods and a minimum commitment of five years.

Recruits will undergo a medical examination and a three-part Initial Strength Test before enlistment. Female recruits must run three-quarters of a mile in 7½ minutes, hold the flexed-arm hang for 13 seconds, and complete 18 sit-ups within one minute.

Recruits will also take a series of tests, including a 10-part aptitude test called the Armed Services Vocational Aptitude Battery (ASVAB). The ASVAB assesses a recruit's academic, verbal, and mathematical abilities, as well as her skills in science, electronics, and mechanics. ASVAB scores also help determine a recruit's job in the Marine Corps.

Why Join?

About 2,000 women join the Marine Corps each year. Why do young women want to be Marines? What motivates them to sign up for the toughest branch of the U. S. military?

Many recruits were influenced by family members who served in the Marines or in another military branch. Most recruits say that they joined the Marine Corps for an exciting challenge.

"This recruit graduated high school and tried different jobs, Sir," explains Private Julia White, 19, of Shetak, Wisconsin. "This recruit felt she was going nowhere with her life, Sir. This recruit had no discipline in her life, Sir.

The Slide for Life tests a recruit's physical strength and her mental toughness.

This recruit liked what the Marines stood for, Sir—the esprit de corps and self-discipline. This recruit can return home with pride, Sir."

Private Erin Hennessey, 18, of Elizabeth, New Jersey, grew up in a military family. She joined the Marine Corps for patriotic reasons. "What happened to those U.S. Marines who were killed in Lebanon [during a 1983 terrorist attack] really affected me," she relates. "It's one of the reasons I wanted to become a Marine."

Preparing for Parris Island

How can a young woman best prepare for the training on Parris Island? What advice would recruits and officers give to those considering enlistment?

"This recruit advises potential recruits to run," says Pamela Jones. "The Marines will build you up when you get here.

Physical fitness is the top priority at boot camp. Recruits have five minutes to complete the obstacle course events, including the log walk, monkey bars, wall scaling, and rope climb. Opposite: early morning PT.

But if you run you'll build up endurance that will help you here. Everything here is motivation and self-motivation."

Lieutenant Colonel Sheryl Murray—commandant of the Fourth Battalion—offers this advice: "The training is very physically demanding. Many of our recruits injure themselves during training, and that is our biggest reason for attrition [dropouts]. During the first three or four days on the island, recruits start with serious PT at 6:30 in the morning. I would advise those considering our training to prepare themselves by getting in good physical condition—before they come here."

Recruits scramble up and down a 25-foot rope — the last event on the obstacle course.

"About 20 to 25 percent of the females coming in are overweight to some degree by our standards," Captain Laura Muhlenberg adds, "and we have to get them on special diets and motivate them to trim down. We see a lot of sportslike injuries: knee, tendon, stress fractures, and some hip injuries. . . . I would advise young women to have a medical checkup and, if your doctor approves, do some serious, regular physical calisthenics and start running gradually—up to three miles a day—before you arrive here."

Captain Catherine Stump, company commander of the Fourth Battalion, agrees: "Don't come here thinking you'll get in shape here. Be in good physical condition when you arrive here, and it will be easier for you. You don't want to be singled out as overweight, or the one unable to get halfway up the rope, or unable to keep up with the rest during basic PT."

"The swimming test presents special problems, especially for our inner-city kids who never learned to swim," points out First Lieutenant Edonna Allen. Officers suggest that recruits without swimming experience take a beginning swimming class before they arrive at Parris Island.

What qualities will help a recruit succeed at Parris Island? "We can work with a physically weak recruit," says First Lieutenant Allen. "We can build that recruit up with physical training and diet. But the critical thing is, in my experience, self-discipline. A recruit coming here has to have some level of this, or they aren't going to make it here.

"It's not that a recruit can't learn self-discipline, it's just that we can't always teach them how to develop it in the short time we have to train them. So some of them are not going to make it for FTA: failure to adjust."

Building self-confidence on the 45-foot rappelling tower

"A successful recruit must join the Marines because she wants to be here," adds Captain Stump. "The more successful recruits here were well-rounded in high school, outgoing, able to work well with others, self-confident, not too self-centered."

A drill instructor comes down hard on a new recruit.

What is the toughest part of being a Marine recruit? Recruits say the House of Pain, the obstacle course, and the conditioning hikes are some of the hardest physical challenges. But the most difficult hurdles at Parris Island are often psychological, especially the stress and adjustments of Phase I.

"Managing stress for the incoming recruit is a major problem area," explains First Lieutenant Allen. "Most have never been yelled at constantly before."

"During the first two weeks you've got three DIs in your face, yelling constantly," concurs Recruit Michelle Wunder of Escanaba, Michigan. "It's hard to stay motivated and live up to their expectations at first. To get through it, I kept telling myself: 'I'm doing this for my country and for myself, and I'm proud of this.'"

53

This sign explains the proper way to knock on a drill instructor's door.

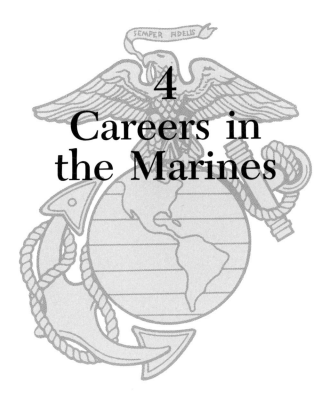

4
Careers in
the Marines

Careers in the Marine Corps resemble many civilian occupations. Career categories, or occupational fields, include accounting, audio-visual support, auditing, aviation, data processing, food service, heavy equipment operations, intelligence, journalism, law, law enforcement, motor transport, personnel administration, public affairs, and weather service.

Each occupational field contains more specific job assignments called military occupation specialties (MOS). Some MOS assignments within avionics, for instance, are mechanics, maintenance, and supply of aircraft. Aviation jobs include weather service, air traffic control, radar, and aerial navigation.

Day Two: Clothing assignments are done production-line style.

A recruit's job assignment and the terms of her enlistment are determined by her ASVAB results. Two important scores, the GT (General Technical) and the AFQT (Armed Forces Qualification Test) scores, are derived from the ASVAB.

General Technical scores help determine a recruit's MOS. A military police position requires a 100-point GT score, for instance, while the more technical job of air traffic controller requires at least 110 points. Job assignments are also determined by which positions are available at the time a recruit enlists. Should competition for a popular MOS develop among a number of candidates, the recruit with the highest GT score would most likely win the job.

The AFQT score is used to determine whether a recruit enlists as a "Bravo" or—with a higher test score—as an "Alpha." Bravos are generally accepted into the Marine Corps on an "open contract." That is, the recruit's occupational field is chosen by the Marine Corps. Alphas, in contrast, can request their own job assignments and their occupational field is often guaranteed—or locked in—upon recruitment. Most recruits (about 80 percent) enter the Marines as Alphas.

Alpha recruits are also eligible for the Quality Enlistment Program, or QEP. The four-year QEP gives a recruit a guaranteed occupational field and the choice of an overseas or an East or West coast assignment after basic training. The six-year QEP adds a guaranteed promotion immediately after basic training (as opposed to six months later for four-year enlistees). Other promotions come sooner as well.

After boot camp, each Marine is assigned to one of more than 500 specialized schools or to a permanent post for on-the-job training. Training periods range from one month to more than a year, depending on the level of knowledge and technical skill required for the job. After specialized training, each Marine is assigned to a stateside or an overseas Marine base. Training schools and Marine bases are all mixed-sex, meaning that men and women train and work together within their occupational fields.

Marines have little free time. Jobs like shining boots keep recruits busy.

Pay and Benefits

As of January 1993, Marines ranked as E1 privates receive $753.60 per month with under four months of service and $814.80 per month after four months. Pay raises occur with each promotion.

Marines receive 30 days of paid leave each year. Other benefits include medical and dental care, prescriptions, room and board (food), an initial set of uniforms, and a clothing allowance of $20 to $30 per month. Officers do not receive a clothing allowance.

The Marine Corps will also help an enlistee pursue a college education after leaving the service. Under the terms of the Montgomery GI Bill, a Marine who sets aside $100 per month for 12 months will later receive money from the government—$300 a month for 36 months—to be used for college expenses.

Becoming an Officer

To be eligible to serve as an officer, a Marine must have a GT score of at least 120 points on the ASVAB. A candidate must also earn a college degree before being commissioned—or named an officer. There are five ways to become an officer in the Marine Corps.

The Naval Academy is a four-year college for U.S. Navy and Marine Corps officers. The Reserve Officers Training Corps (ROTC) is an officer-training program operated at most major American universities. A college education through either the Naval Academy or the ROTC is paid for by the United States government. Both programs are difficult to enter, however—only students with outstanding academic records are admitted.

College students who aren't enrolled in ROTC may become Marine officers by entering the Platoon Leader Course after their junior year of college. The Officer Candidates Class (OCC) is a 10-week course for Marines who have already graduated from college and are under 28 years old.

An enlisted Marine whose performance is outstanding may qualify to become an officer under the Marine Corps Enlisted Commissioning Program. Those Marines selected for the program attend college and OCC.

Graduates of all officer-training programs are commissioned as second lieutenants. After their commission, officers receive six months of officer training at the Basic School in Quantico, Virginia.

At one time, women held only clerical positions in the Marine Corps.
Now they prepare for combat just like the men.

5
Women in the Marines:
A Growing Role

The Marine Corps was created on November 10, 1775—just seven months after the start of the American Revolution and one month after the creation of the Navy. America's founders intended the Navy and the Marine Corps to work together. The Navy would guard America's interests at sea, and the Marines would be an amphibious assault and strike force capable of moving from Navy ships to enemy shores on short notice.

The Marine Corps was an all-male service until World War I (1914–1918). About 300 women served in the Marines during the war—mostly in clerical positions. After the war, all the women were issued "separation orders"—that is, they were discharged.

The changing face of women in the Marine Corps. Bottom right: A female Marine and her male counterpart, World War I. Bottom left: Marines arrive at the U.S. Marine Corps Air Station in Oahu, Hawaii, in the early 1950s. Left: Recruits learn to apply camouflage grease during Basic Warrior Training, 1992.

The Marine Corps Women's Reserve was created on November 7, 1942—less than a year after the United States entered World War II. About 18,000 female Marines served in clerical, recruiting, and air traffic control positions during the war. The Marine Corps used a slogan—Free a Man to Fight—to recruit women for noncombat jobs.

Although the Marine Corps encouraged women to enlist for patriotic reasons in wartime, it discouraged women from pursuing military careers during peacetime. "The American tradition is that a woman's place is in the home," stated Brigadier General Gerald C. Thomas in 1945. "Women do not take kindly to military regimentation." By the end of World War II, fewer than 100 female Marines were still on active duty.

Thomas's view was not shared by everyone, though. In 1948, under pressure from military and civilian women, Congress passed the Women's Armed Forces Integration Act, requiring the military to enlist women on active duty status in all branches. But the act barred women from performing any military job that involved combat.

By the 1960s, the image of the Marine Corps as an all-male fighting force was changing. Approximately 2,700 female Marines took part in the Vietnam War during the late 1960s and early 1970s.

While all noncombat jobs were open to them in theory, bias and discrimination often prevented female soldiers from holding jobs—like mechanic, radar operator, and navigator—that were traditionally performed only by men. In 1972 Congress passed a law stating that women could not be denied acceptance into any occupational field in the military, other than combat-related assignments.

Women and Combat

The military's ban on women in combat has been controversial. People who favor the ban claim that women lack the physical and emotional strength required of a soldier in combat. Opponents of the law contest this claim, arguing that the ban unfairly discriminates against women.

When the United States Army invaded Panama in 1989, several military policewomen came under enemy attack.

64

Their performance under fire proved that women are capable combat soldiers and helped put pressure on the military to change its policies.

As demonstrated in Panama, the lines between combat and noncombat assignments are often unclear. Thus, the Marine Corps has improved its training programs to better prepare women for assignments near the front line of battle. In October 1989, the Marines made Basic Warrior Training a requirement for all female recruits. The only Basic Warrior Training activities that women do not take part in are pugil stick exercises—in which recruits batter one another with a padded staff—and boxing.

In 1991 more than 33,300 women, including more than 2,000 Marines, served in Operation Desert Storm—the Persian Gulf War. Female Marines held positions in communications, surveillance, reconnaissance, and intelligence. Some drove trucks and delivered supplies behind enemy lines. Others transported prisoners of war (POWs) back to allied territory.

Women in the combined military branches flew jets and helicopters, directed artillery fire, and ran POW camps. Female soldiers served on support and repair ships, in port security units, and in construction battalions. One Army woman, who was nicknamed "SCUD Buster," worked at a computer station in Saudi Arabia, launching Patriot missiles to intercept and destroy incoming Iraqi SCUD missiles.

Technically women performed "support," not combat, assignments in the Persian Gulf. Nevertheless, many women encountered combat situations. Female pilots flew Chinook helicopters, delivering supplies and picking up wounded soldiers during the conflict. Two Army women were taken prisoner when their helicopter crashed during a rescue operation. Fourteen women lost their lives in the war.

The outstanding performance of women in the Persian Gulf helped dispel old myths about physical strength limitations and women's stability under fire. The performance of America's servicewomen earned them the respect of their superiors, their male counterparts, and the public.

With strong support in Congress and public opinion polls for the military to widen the role of women in combat-related assignments, President George Bush established the Presidential Commission on the Assignment of Women in the Armed Forces in March 1992. This 15-member group (9 men and 6 women) was asked to advise the president on the laws and military policies relating to women and to assess whether the combat exclusion clauses for women were equitable.

The commission presented its findings to President Bush on November 15, 1992. Commission members opposed the assignment of women to ground combat positions—such as those in infantry, armor, and artillery units—noting several concerns. Commission members felt that physical strength limits might impede women in combat, that mixed-sex combat units might not work together as a cohesive team, and that female prisoners of war might be victims of rape and other tortures.

On the other hand, the commission recommended that the role of women in combat-related support assignments be expanded in all services, provided that women meet the physical standards (for strength and stamina) required to perform the jobs in question. The commission noted that women already serve in combat-related positions in Air

During inspections belt buckles must sparkle.

Although female Marines are not trained as frontline troops, the Marine Corps wants women to be ready for combat situations.

Force missile silos, Army air defense units, and other support units that have been exposed to enemy fire in recent years.

On April 28, 1993, Defense Secretary Les Aspin significantly expanded the opportunities for women in the military. Aspin ordered the armed forces to drop most restrictions on women in aerial and naval combat. Women are now eligible to fly aircraft in combat and to serve on warships. Secretary Aspin also ordered the military services to justify any jobs that still remain off-limits to women.

In keeping with the secretary's order, the Marine Corps, which previously barred women from aviation altogether,

announced that qualified women would be eligible to apply for positions as aircraft pilots and aircraft crew members. In addition, the Marine Corps announced it would begin studying additional opportunities for women to serve in ground combat units. The units under consideration are those with a low probability of combat engagement, such as field artillery and air defense.

With the role of women in the military growing, this is an exciting time to become a Marine. Women who choose military service as a career—in the Marines and in other military branches—will continue to find new opportunities opening up to them, especially in combat-related assignments.

The Marines are looking for a few extraordinary young women. Those women who successfully pass through Parris Island, regardless of their chosen path after military service, will leave with a firm new foundation of self-confidence and discipline. They will have gained a sense of personal achievement that will stay with them for the rest of their lives.

Private Patricia Marquez has earned the right to be called a Marine. She gets a hug from her sister (right) after the Emblem Ceremony.

Index